Music Minus One Bass-Baritone

4066

BASS-BARITONE OPERA ARIAS WITH ORCHESTRA

Volume 2

RACHMANINOV: Aleko *Aleko's cavatina (Aleko)*

GOUNOD: Faust
Vous qui faites l'endormie (Mephistopheles)

BEETHOVEN: Fidelio
Hat man nicht auch Gold daneben (Rocco)

MOZART: Le Nozze di Figaro *Non più andrai (Figaro)*

MOZART: Don Giovanni
Madamina! Il catalogo è questo (Leporelo)

Suggestions for using this MMO edition

We have tried to create a product that will provide you an easy way to learn and perform a concerto with a full orchestra in the comfort of your own home. Because it involves a fixed orchestral performance, there is an inherent lack of flexibility in tempo and cadenza length. The following MMO features and techniques will reduce these inflexibilities and help you maximize the effectiveness of the MMO practice and performance system:

Regarding tempi: again, we have observed generally accepted tempi, but some may wish to perform at a different tempo, or to slow down or speed up the accompaniment for practice purposes. You can purchase from MMO (or from other audio and electronics dealers) specialized CD players which allow variable speed in combination while maintaining proper pitch. This is an indispensable tool for the serious musician and you may wish to look into purchasing this useful piece of equipment for full enjoyment of all your MMO editions.

We want to provide you with the most useful practice and performance accompaniments possible. If you have any suggestions for improving the MMO system, please feel free to contact us. You can reach us by e-mail at mmogroup@musicminusone.com.

Music Minus One

4066

BASS-BARITONE OPERA ARIAS WITH ORCHESTRA

VOLUME II

MMO 4066

4

A Note on the Arias

Sergei Rachmaninov achieved quite a feat when he composed his opera *Aleko* at the grand old age of nineteen at the end of his college career. That this opera should have also carved itself a place in the international repertoire is doubly amazing, though it is only in recent years that the piece has been performed to any extent in Western Europe or America. It is spellbinding music, and Rachmaninov shows that at this young age he had a complete understanding of voice against orchestra, and indeed of the complex nature of opera itself.

Aleko is cast in a single act, and indeed this was prerequisite to the piece's composition. Rachmaninov's impetus was that of his final exam at the Moscow Conservatory. It came in the form of a competition between himself and two other students in Anton Arensky's composition class to compose a one-act opera on a given text. It so happened that the Italian megahit *Cavalleria Rusticana* was very popular in Russia in the early 1890s and this no doubt had an impact on the decision of the text which was given the three young men: a libretto by Vladimir Nemirovich-Danchenko from Pushkin's poem *The Gypsies*. Its structure and theme is very much reminiscent of *Cavalleria*, though *Aleko's* structure is not as well worked-out; in fact this made Rachmaninov's job all the harder, to unify with music what was a somewhat fragmented dramatic text.

But so successful was Rachmaninov in his effort (he completed it in three weeks!) that he won the competition and was given a special honor: the Great Golden Medal. Needless to say, he graduated.

The opera was not finally performed until 27 April 1893, with none other than Tchaikovsky cheering as the curtain dropped. This was an auspicious career-launching for a magnificent talent.

The cavatina presented here is a highlight of the opera, and its fame is due in no small measure to Rachmaninov's good friend Fyodor Chaliapin, who performed the role many times and who brought Rachmaninov's characteristic broad melodic phrases to their maximum effect.

Faust

Gounod's *Faust* is of course one of the standards in the French (and international) operatic repertoire, one which audiences always enjoy and which contains a remarkably rich palette of musical material.

Charles-François Gounod was born 17 June 1818 in Paris. He was a very religious and spiritual man, and one devoted to classical ideals; as a young man he was set for the priesthood and it was the great French singer Pauline Viardot who convinced him otherwise. His beliefs cast a heavy influence over his works, and it is only fitting that he should bring to life the classic Faust tale in an operatic setting, and to do it so admirably.

For operatic purposes, Gounod and librettists Jules Barbier and Michel Carré based the opera on both Goethe's 1808 play and Carré's own *Faust and Marguerite*. The project was urged to completion by Léon Carvalho, director of the Théâtre Lyrique, who was anxious for a vehicle for his wife, the singer Marie Carvalho (and indeed it was she who filled Marguerite's shoes at the première on 19 March 1859). Mephistopheles was portrayed by basso Emile Balanqué.

The magnificent aria "Vous qui faites l'endormie" occurs in Act Four, as Mephistopheles makes a grotesque parody of Faust's love for Marguerite, in the form of a mock serenade to Marguerite at her window. Gounod's masterful orchestration makes the aria extremely effective and unsettling.

The opera was of course a great success and became enormously successful abroad, where it has been translated into several languages; Gounod even added an aria for its 1864 English-language première in London. The opera became popular in Germany under the title *Margarethe* (to avoid comparison with Goethe's famous original). Gounod would go on to compose the enormously popular *Romeo et Juliette*, and until his death on 18 October 1893 at Saint-Cloud outside Paris, Gounod remained one of the most respected of all operatic composers.

FIDELIO

Beethoven's *Fidelio* (or *Leonore,* as Beethoven preferred to title it) had a rocky road between its initial genesis in 1804 and its "final" première on 23 May 1814. The composer, who had such facility in composing instrumental works, was quite desperate to compose an opera. However, the scope of such a project, and perhaps his unfamiliarity with the multifaceted problems opera presented, took a tortuous route. After two failed productions, in 1805 and 1806, Beethoven's revisions would culminate in the heavily improved and successful 1814 version with which we are familiar today.

The story involves a woman, Leonore, whose husband, Florestan, has been imprisoned by a political enemy, Pizarro, and is believed dead. In search of Florestan, she disguises herself as a man, Fidelio, and infiltrates Pizarro's prison. The aria "Hat man nicht auch Gold beineben" takes place in Act One as Rocco, the jailer, espouses the importance of money in marriage to Fidelio/Leonore, who he suspects is interested romantically in his daughter.

It is a relatively brief and lighthearted but masterful aria, and one which adds much to the overall character of *Fidelio*, which despite its troubled genesis has established itself for roughly two centuries in the international repertoire.

LE NOZZE DI FIGARO

Many feel that Mozart's most magnificent opera is *Le Nozze di Figaro*, which premièred on 1 May 1786 in Vienna. Its sophisticated hilarity, brought to perfection by Lorenzo da Ponte's libretto, managed at that time, as it does now, to appeal to people rich and poor, educated or not. Its cleverness owes much to a climate of censorship violations (Beaumarchais' play, which formed the basis for the opera, had been banned by the Emperor, who grudgingly gave permission for Mozart and librettist da Ponte to produce it).

"Non più andrai" comes at the finale of Act One, in the form of a spirited warning from Figaro to Cherubino (who has been hastened away for military service by the jealous Count) regarding the sobering realities of a soldier's life in comparison with his recent amorous exploits. It is one of the opera's high points and a magnificent display for the basso.

DON GIOVANNI

Mozart's operatic masterpiece *Don Giovanni,* which premièred in Prague on 29 October 1787, is a dark retelling of the Don Juan legend that shows Mozart at his mature pinnacle. Mozart used his trusted librettist Lorenzo da Ponte for this "lighthearted drama" which indeed manages to have its frivolous moments; but it is the serious side of this tale (its complete title was *Il dissoluto punito, ossia Il Don Giovanni*) and Mozart's monumental music, which leaves the final impression.

"Madamina! Il catologo è questo" takes place in Act One as Leporello, Don Giovanni's manservant, tells Donna Elvira, one of his master's victims, of his master's many conquests (2065!). It is a magnificent and memorable aria with a memorable alternating fast-slow tempo and a great display for a rich basso voice. It is Mozart at his most brilliantly vibrant and vital.

Don Giovanni's première at the Nationaltheater in Prague on 29 October 1787 was an undisputed triumph. And in the more than 200 years that have ensued, it has quite deservedly never lost its place in the pantheon of great operas.

—*Michael Norell*

ALEKO

ALEKO'S CAVATINA

Sergei Rachmaninov
(1873-1943)

8

та - ла мне о - на тог-да: „Люб-лю те-бя! В тво-ей я
-ta - la mne o - na tog-da: "Lyub-lyu te-bya! V tvo-eyi ya

вла - сти! Тво-я, А-ле-ко, на-всег-да!"
vla - sti! Tvo-ya, A-le-ko, na-vseg-da!"

Con moto

И всё тог-да я за-бы-вал,
I vso tog-da ya za-bui-val,

12

ког - да   ре - чам е - ё вни - мал
Kog - da   re - cham e - o vni - mal

п, как бе - зум - ный, це - ло - вал   е - ё   ча -
i, kak ve - zum - nyiy, tse - lo - val   e - o   cha -

- ру - ю - щи е о - чи,   кос чуд - ных прядь, тем - не - е
- ru - yu - shti - e o - chi,   kos chud - nyikh pryada, tem - ne - e

MMO 4066

14

MMO 4066

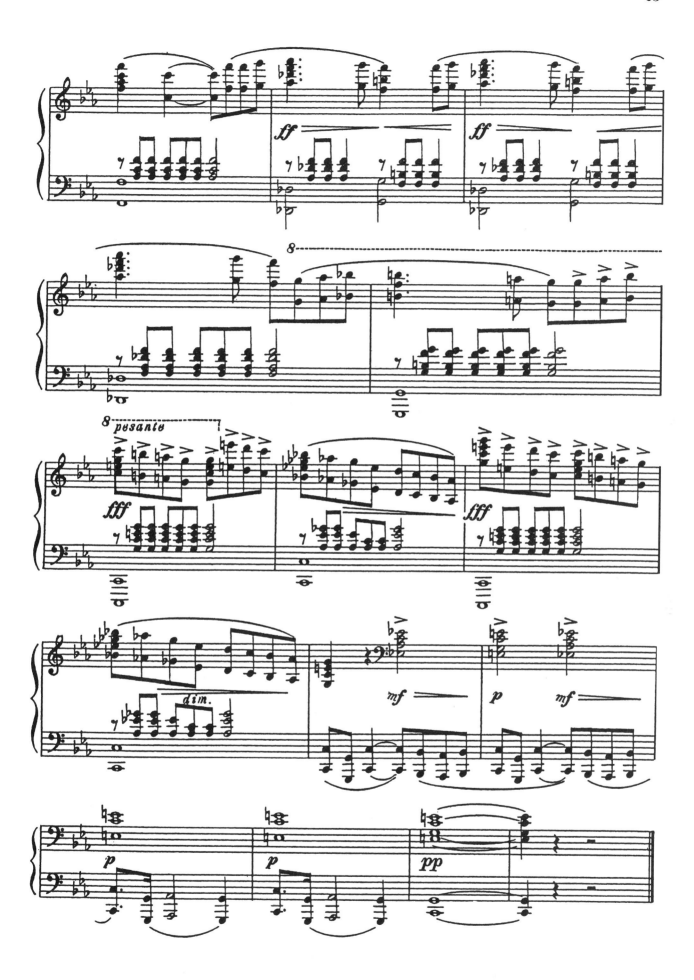

FAUST

Vous qui faites l'endormie

Charles Gounod
(1818-1893)

Ain-si ton galant t'ap-pel - le,__ ain-si ton ga-lant t'ap-pel - le__

Et ton cœur l'en croit! Ah! ah! ah! ah! ah! ah! ah! ah! ah! ah!

N'ouvre ta por-te, ma bel - le, Que la bague au__ doigt, N'ou -

- vre ta por-te, ma bel-le, Que la bague au doigt, que la bague au doigt!

18

MMO 4066

FIDELIO

HAT MAN NICHT AUCH GOLD DANEBEN

Ludwig van Beethoven
(1770-1827)

Hat man nicht auch Gold da-ne-ben kann man nicht ganz glück-lich sein; trau-rig schleppt sich fort das Le-ben, man-cher Kum-mer stellt sich ein, man - cher Kum-mer stellt sich ein.

22

Tempo I.

Das Glück dient wie ein Knecht für Sold, es ist ein schö-nes, schö-nes Ding, das

Gold, das Gold, es ist ein schö - nes Ding, das

Gold, ein gold-nes, gold - - nes Ding, das Gold, das Gold.

Wenn sich Nichts mit Nichts ver -

bin-det, ist und bleibt die Sum-me klein; wer bei
If you

MMO 4066

24

Le Nozze di Figaro

Non più andrai

Wolfgang Amadeus Mozart
(1756-1791)

26

mor.

Non più a-

vrai que-sti bei pennac-chi - ni,

quel ca-

pel - lo leg-gie - ro ga-lan-te,

quel-la chio-ma,quell'a - ria bril-

lan - te,

quel ver - mi - glio don-ne - sco co - lor,

quel ver-

mi - glio don - ne - sco co - lor.

Non più a-

28

po - so, Nar - ci - set - to, A - don - ci - no d'a - mor.

Fra guer - rie - ri, pof - far Bac - co!

Gran mustac - chi, stret - to

sac - co, schiop - po in spal - la, scia - bla al fian - co, col - lo

drit - to, mu - so franco, un gran ca - sco, un gran tur - ban - te, molto o-

nor, po - co con - tan - te, po - co con - tan - te, po - co con - tan - te, ed in-

vrai   quei pen-nac-chi-ni,   non più a-

vrai   quel ca-pel-lo,   non più a-

vrai   quel-la chio-ma,   non più a-

vrai   quell'a-ria bril-lan-te. Non più avrai, far-fallone a-mo-ro-so,   notte e

giorno d'in-tor-no gi-ran-do,   del-le bel-le tur-bando il ri-po-so, Narci-

set - to, Adon - ci - no d'a - mor, del - le bel - le tur - bando il ri -

po - so, Nar - ci - set - to, A - don - ci - no d'a - mor.

Che - ru - bino al - la vit - to - ria, al - la gloria mi - li -

tar, Che - ru - bi - no al - la vit - to - ria, al - la

glo - ria mi - li - tar, al - la glo - ria mi - li -

al - la glo - ria mi - li - tar!

Don Giovanni

Madamina! il catologo è questo!

Wolfgang Amadeus Mozart
(1756-1791)

Allegro LEPORELLO

Ma-da-mi - na! Il ca-ta - lo-go è

que - sto, Del-le bel - le, che a-mò il pa-dron mi - o, Un ca-

ta - - lo-go e gli è, che ho fat-to i - o, Os-ser-

va - te, leg - ge - te con me! Os - ser-

va - te, leg - ge - te con me!

In I - ta - lia sei-cen - to e qua-

ran - ta; In Al - magna due-cen - to e tren-

t'u - na, Cen - to in Francia, in Turchia novan-

t'u - na; Ma in I - spa-gna, ma in I - spa-gna son già mille e tre!

mil-le e tre, mil-le e tre! V'han fra queste con-ta-
di - ne, Ca - me - rie - re, ci - ta - di - ne, V'han con-tes-se, ba - ro -
nes - se, Mar-che-sa - ne, prin-ci - pes-se; E v'han don-ne d'o-gni
gra - do, D'o - gni for - ma, d'o - gni e - tà! d'o - gni

38

for - ma,   d'o - gnie - tà!   d'o - gni

for - ma,   d'o - gnie - tà!

Andante con moto.

Nel - la bion-da e - gli ha l'u - san-za Di lo - dar - la

la gen - ti - lez - za,   Nel - la bru - na

la co - stan-za,   Nel - la bian - ca

la _____ dol - cez - za.   Vuol d'in - ver - - no la gras-

sot - - ta, Vuol d'es - ta - - te la ma-grot-ta,   E la

gran-de   ma - e - sto - sa,   E la

gran - - de   ma - e - sto - - - - -

42

OPERA with ORCHESTRA

Music Minus One is proud to present the finest arias in the operatic repertoire—now available with full orchestral accompaniment! We have brought the finest European vocalists and orchestras together to create an unparalleled experience—giving you the opportunity to sing opera the way it was meant to be performed. All titles are now CD+Graphics encoded so you can see the lyrics on your television screen in real-time—and, as always, the full printed vocal score is included as well.

Soprano

SOPRANO ARIAS WITH ORCHESTRA
Zvetelina Maldjanska – Vidin Philharmonic/Todorov   MMO CDG 4052

Puccini – La Bohème *Mi chiamano Mimi (Mimi)*; Mozart – Die Zauberflöte *Ach, ich fühl's*; Verdi – I Vespri Siciliani *Siciliana d'Elena*; Bizet – Les Pêcheurs de Perles *Me voilà seule dans la nuit*; Meyerbeer – Dinorah *Ombre légère qui suis mes pas (Shadow song) (Dinorah)*

SOPRANO ARIAS WITH ORCHESTRA
Ljudmila Gerova – Festival Orchestra of Bulgaria/Todorov   MMO CDG 4054

W.A. Mozart - Recitative and Aria *Ergo Interest, an quis...Quære Superna*, KV. 143; Mozart - Le Nozze di Figaro *Venite, inginocchiatevi (Susanna)*; Mozart – Le Nozze di Figaro *Giunse alfin il momento...Deh Vieni, non tardar (Susanna)*; C.M. v.Weber – Der Freischütz *Und ob die Wolke sie verhülle*; Puccini – Tosca *Vissi d'arte, vissi d'amore*

BELLINI OPERA SCENES AND ARIAS FOR SOPRANO AND ORCHESTRA
Zvetelina Maldjanska – Plovdiv Philharmonic/Todorov   MMO CDG 4063

Norma *Casta diva...Fine al rito...Ah! bello a mi ritorna (Norma)*; I Puritani *Qui la voce sua soave...Vien, diletto (Elvira).*

LA SONNAMBULA: SCENES AND ARIAS FOR SOPRANO AND ORCHESTRA
Zvetelina Maldjanska – Plovdiv Philharmonic/Todorov   MMO CDG 4064

Care compagne...A te, diletta, tenera madre...Come per me sereno..Sovra il sen (Amina); Ah! Se una volta sola...Ah! non credea mirarti...Ah! Non giunge (Amina)

DONIZETTI SOPRANO SCENES & ARIAS WITH ORCHESTRA
Zvetelina Maldjanska – Plovdiv Philharmonic/Todorov   MMO CDG 4058

Don Pasquale – Act I, Scene 4 *Quel guardo il cavaliere...So anch'io la virtù magica (Norina)*; Lucia di Lammermoor – Act I, Scene 2: *Quella fonte... – Regnava nel silenzio – Quando rapito in estasi (Lucia)*; Lucia di Lammermoor – Act II, Scene 5 *Il dolce suono – Ardon gl'Incensi – Alfin son tua – spargi d'amaro pianto (Lucia)*

MOZART OPERA ARIAS FOR SOPRANO AND ORCHESTRA
Zvetelina Maldjanska – Plovdiv Philharmonic/Todorov   MMO CDG 4060

Don Giovanni *In quali eccessi, o Numi...Mi tradì quell' alma ingrata (Donna Elvira)*; Die Zauberflöte *Ach, ich fühl's, es ist verschwunden (Pamina)*; Le Nozze di Figaro *E Susanna non vien!...Dove sono I bei momenti (Contessa)*; Le Nozze di Figaro *Giunse alfin il momento...Deh Vieni, non tardar (Susanna)*; Die Entführung aus dem Serail *Martern aller Arten (Constanze)*

MOZART OPERA ARIAS FOR SOPRANO AND ORCHESTRA, VOLUME II
Snejana Dramtcheva - Plovdiv Philharmonic/Todorov   MMO CDG 4065

Die Zauberflöte *O zitt're nicht, mein lieber Sohn...Zum Leiden bin ich auserkoren (Queen of the Night)*; Die Entführung aus dem Serail *Durch Zärtlichkeit und Schmeicheln (Blonde)*; Die Entführung aus dem Serail *Welche Wonne, welche Lust herrscht nun mehr in meiner Brust (Blonde)*; Così fan tutte *Una donna a quindici anni (Despina)*; Don Giovanni *Batti, batti, o bel Masetto (Zerlina)*; Don Giovanni *Vedrai, carino, se sei buonino (Zerlina)*

PUCCINI SOPRANO ARIAS WITH ORCHESTRA
Zvetelina Maldjanska – Plovdiv Philharmonic Orchestra/Todorov   MMO CDG 4053

La Bohème *Mi chiamano Mimi (Mimi)*; La Bohème *Quando me'n vo' soletta la via" (Musetta)*; La Bohème *Donde lieta (Mimi)*; Gianni Schicchi – *O mio babbino caro (Lauretta)*; Turanodot *Signore, ascolta! (Liù)*; Turanodot *Tu che di gel sei cinta (Liù)*

VERDI SOPRANO OPERA ARIAS WITH ORCHESTRA
Zvetelina Maldjanska – Plovdiv Philharmonic/Todorov   MMO CDG 4059

La Traviata *È strano! È strano!…Ah fors'è lui che l'anima solinga ne' tumulti…Follie! Sempre libera (Violetta)*; I Vespri Siciliani *(Siciliana d'Elena) Mercè, dilette amiche (Elena)*; Falstaff *Sul fil d'un soffio etesio (Nannetta)*; Otello *Piangea cantando (The Willow Song) (Desdemona)*; Rigoletto *Caro nome (Gilda)*; La Traviata – Scene *Attendo, attendo…* and aria *Addio del passato (Violetta)*

VERDI MEZZO-SOPRANO ARIAS WITH ORCHESTRA
Ivanka Ninova – Festival Orchestra of Bulgaria/Todorov   MMO CDG 4055

Il Trovatore *Condotta ell'era in ceppi (Azucena)*; Il Trovatore *Stride la vampa! (Azucena)*; Don Carlo *O don fatale (Eboli)*; Don Carlo *Nei giardin del bello (Eboli)*; Nabucco *Oh, dischiuso, è il firmamento (Fenena)*

FRENCH & ITALIAN OPERA ARIAS FOR MEZZO-SOPRANO AND ORCHESTRA
Ivanka Ninova – Plovdiv Philharmonic/Todorov   MMO CDG 4062

Bizet – Carmen *L'amour est un oiseau rebelle (La Havanaise) (Carmen)*; Saint-Saëns – Samson et Dalila *Samson, recherchant ma présence (Dalila)*; Cilea – Adriana Lecouvreur *Acerba volutta…Ognieco, ogni ombra...O vagabonda stella d'Oriente (La Principessa)*; Ponchielli – La Gioconda *Voce di donna o d'angelo (Cieca)*; Mascagni – Cavalleria Rusticana *Voi lo sapete, o mama (Santuzza)*; Donizetti – *La Favorita Fia dunque vero? (Leonora)*

ITALIAN TENOR ARIAS WITH ORCHESTRA
Kamen Tchanev – Plovdiv Philharmonic/Todorov   MMO CDG 4057

Puccini – La Bohème *Che gelida manina (Rodolfo)*; Puccini – Tosca *Recondita armonia (Cavaradossi)*; Donizetti – L'Elisir d'Amore *Una furtiva lagrima (Nemorino)*; Verdi – Rigoletto *La donna è mobile (Duca)*; Verdi – La Traviata scene and aria: *Lunge da Lei…De' miei bollenti spiriti (Alfredo)*

PUCCINI ARIAS FOR TENOR AND ORCHESTRA
Vesselin Hristov – Plovdiv Philharmonic Orchestra/Todorov   MMO CDG 4061

Turandot *Nessun dorma! (Calaf)*; Turandot *Non piangere, Liù! (Il Principe)*; Tosca *Recondita armonia (Cavaradossi)*; Tosca *E lucevan le stelle (Cavaradossi)*; Madama Butterfly *Addio, Fiorito asil (Pinkerton)*; Manon Lescaut *Donna non vidi mai simile a questa! (Des Grieux)*; La Bohème *Che gelida manina (Rodolfo)*

BASS-BARITONE ARIAS WITH ORCHESTRA
Ivaylo Djourov – Festival Orchestra of Bulgaria/Todorov   MMO CDG 4056

Mozart – Le Nozze di Figaro *Vedrò mentr'io sospiro (Il Conte)*; Mozart – Le Nozze di Figaro *Se vuol ballare, signor contino (Figaro)*; Rossini – Il Barbiere di Siviglia *La callunia è un venticello (Basilio)*; Verdi – Simon Boccanegra *Il lacerato spirito (Fiesco)*; Puccini – La Bohème *Vecchia zimarra (Colline)*

For the entire Opera with Orchestra catalogue visit MMO on the web at
WWW.MUSICMINUSONE.COM

TO ORDER BY PHONE CALL 1-800-669-7464 (U.S.) • 914-592-1188 (INTERNATIONAL)

The John Wustman Series of Vocal Recordings

In a field dominated by the vocal soloist, John Wustman is one of the few accompanists in this country who has achieved renown and critical acclaim in this most challenging of art forms. Mr. Wustman has developed that rare quality of bringing a strength and character to his accompaniments which create a true collaboration between the singer and the pianist. And this is as it should be, for in the art song especially the piano part is not mere rhythmic and tonal background, but an integral part of the composer's intent and creation. Thus, on these recordings, Mr. Wustman provides not only the necessary accompaniment but also through his artistry, stylistic and interpretive suggestion for the study of the music.

Among the many artists he has accompanied in past years are Montserrat Caballe, Regine Crespin, Nicolai Gedda, Anna Moffo, Birgit Nilsson, Jan Peerce, Roberta Peters, Elisabeth Schwarzkopf, Renata Scotto and William Warfield.

Mr. Wustman has become known to millions of television viewers as the accompanist to Luciano Pavarotti in his many appearances in that medium.

Lieder

BRAHMS GERMAN LIEDER for High Voice ....MMO CD 4005
SCHUBERT GERMAN LIEDER for High Voice, Vol. 1...........MMO CD 4001
SCHUBERT GERMAN LIEDER for High Voice, Vol. 2 ....MMO CD 4003
SCHUMANN GERMAN LIEDER for High Voice ....MMO CD 4024
STRAUSS GERMAN LIEDER for High Voice ....MMO CD 4022
WOLF GERMAN LIEDER for High Voice ....MMO CD 4020
17th/18th CENT. ITALIAN SONGS for High Voice, Vol. 1 ......MMO CD 4011
17th/18th CENT. ITALIAN SONGS for High Voice, Vol. 2 ......MMO CD 4013
EVERYBODY'S FAVORITE SONGS for High Voice, Vol. 1 ...MMO CD 4007
EVERYBODY'S FAVORITE SONGS for High Voice, Vol. 2 ...MMO CD 4009

BRAHMS GERMAN LIEDER for Low Voice ....MMO CD 4006
SCHUBERT GERMAN LIEDER for Low Voice, Vol. 1 ....MMO CD 4002
SCHUBERT GERMAN LIEDER for Low Voice, Vol. 2 ....MMO CD 4004
SCHUMANN GERMAN LIEDER for Low Voice ....MMO CD 4025
STRAUSS GERMAN LIEDER for Low Voice ....MMO CD 4023
WOLF GERMAN LIEDER for Low Voice ....MMO CD 4021
17th/18th CENT. ITALIAN SONGS for Low Voice, Vol. 1 ....MMO CD 4012
17th/18th CENT. ITALIAN SONGS for Low Voice, Vol. 2 ....MMO CD 4014
EVERYBODY'S FAVORITE SONGS for Low Voice, Vol. 1 ....MMO CD 4008
EVERYBODY'S FAVORITE SONGS for Low Voice, Vol. 2 ....MMO CD 4010

Arias

FAMOUS SOPRANO ARIAS ....MMO CD 4015
MOZART ARIAS FOR SOPRANO ....MMO CD 4026
VERDI ARIAS FOR SOPRANO ....MMO CD 4027
ITALIAN ARIAS FOR SOPRANO ....MMO CD 4028
FRENCH ARIAS FOR SOPRANO ....MMO CD 4029
ORATORIO ARIAS FOR SOPRANO ....MMO CD 4030

FAMOUS MEZZO-SOPRANO ARIAS ....MMO CD 4016

ORATORIO ARIAS FOR ALTO ....MMO CD 4031

FAMOUS TENOR ARIAS ....MMO CD 4017
ORATORIO ARIAS FOR TENOR ....MMO CD 4032

FAMOUS BARITONE ARIAS ....MMO CD 4018

FAMOUS BASS ARIAS ....MMO CD 4019
ORATORIO ARIAS FOR BASS ....MMO CD 4033

Laureate Series Contest Solos

BEGINNING SOPRANO SOLOS KATE HURNEY/BRUCE EBERLE.....................MMO CD 4041
INTERMEDIATE SOPRANO SOLOS KATE HURNEY/BRUCE EBERLE...........................MMO CD 4042

BEGINNING MEZZO-SOPRANO SOLOS FAY KITTELSON/RICHARD FOSTER ....MMO CD 4043
INTERMEDIATE MEZZO-SOPRANO SOLOS FAY KITTELSON/RICHARD FOSTER ....MMO CD 4044
ADVANCED MEZZO-SOPRANO SOLOS FAY KITTELSON/RICHARD FOSTER.............MMO CD 4045

BEGINNING CONTRALTO SOLOS CARLINE RAY/BRUCE EBERLE ....MMO CD 4046

BEGINNING TENOR SOLOS GEORGE SHIRLEY/WAYNE SANDERS ....MMO CD 4047
INTERMEDIATE TENOR SOLOS GEORGE SHIRLEY/WAYNE SANDERS ....MMO CD 4048
ADVANCED TENOR SOLOS GEORGE SHIRLEY/WAYNE SANDERS...........................MMO CD 4049

TWELVE CLASSIC VOCAL STANDARDS, VOL.1 ....MMO CD 4050
TWELVE CLASSIC VOCAL STANDARDS, VOL.2 ....MMO CD 4051

AVAILABLE FROM FINE MUSIC AND RECORD DEALERS
OR VISIT US AT WWW.MUSICMINUSONE.COM
TO ORDER BY PHONE CALL 1-800-669-7464 (U.S.) • 914-592-1188 (INT'L)

MUSIC MINUS ONE
50 Executive Boulevard
Elmsford, New York 10523-1325
800-669-7464 (U.S.)/914-592-1188 (International)

www.musicminusone.com
e-mail: mmogroup@musicminusone.com

MMO 4066